GOOD MORNING, LORD

Devotions for Young Teens

Greta Rey

BAKER BOOK HOUSE

Grand Rapids, Michigan 49506

To **Doris**
who was my little sister
and is now my best friend

Special thanks to my mother and sister
for their help and encouragement

Copyright 1983 by
Baker Book House Company

ISBN: 0–8010–7719–2

Printed in the United States of America

1. THE WHOLE REASON FOR ME

READ: Ephesians 1:1–14.

"Why did God make me?" you wonder, usually when life seems unbearable. The question and its answer are basic to our belief about God and life.

God is the reason for everything. He made all things so they would praise and honor Him. People can understand that reason for their existence.

God is love. God made all living things, particularly people, to love Him. But love is a giving relationship, so God made all things to receive His love as well.

The human being is the creature God created to be most like Him, to reflect His loving self. People can receive and respond to God's love by loving Him, just as He receives and responds to their love. They also reflect God's love through their loving relationships with each other.

"Where does *my* happiness come in?" you may wonder. It's simple. Happiness comes from being what you are meant to be. People are happiest when they are loving and praising God and loving other people.

Sin is being the opposite of what you're intended to be. It is self-centeredness and self-love that excludes love of God and neighbor. Any sin fits this definition. Trying to be what you were not intended to be makes you, and usually other people, unhappy.

The good news of course is that our happiness has been restored. God loves us and wants us to be happy, so He made us perfect through Christ. Christ wiped out our sin and its results and restored us to be the loving, praising creatures we are meant to be—forever.

Praise the Lord!

2. WHAT IS AN ADOLESCENT?

READ: Psalm 148.

An adolescent is a person
> between childhood and adulthood, who can have the best of both worlds, but often gets the worst.
>
> whose new voice is tricky.
>
> who can't wait to turn 16.
>
> whose daydreams are giving way to a reality that's within reach.
>
> who dreams of being a star, but is deeply satisfied with just being liked.
>
> who tries to be noticed, and is embarrassed about being the center of attention.
>
> who says crazy things without thinking, and worries later about the impression those comments made.
>
> who wails, "Nobody understands me," and silently thinks, "Neither do I."
>
> who thinks parents are impossible.
>
> who has super energy, and can get super-tired.
>
> who can be totally carefree, and totally scared.
>
> who no longer regards the opposite sex as a carrier of "cooties" but as a tantalizing mystery.

An adolescent is important to his family.

An adolescent is important to God—created by Him, loved by Him, saved by Him.

An adolescent is growing on the schedule that God created in every human being.

God understands the problems of youth while He admires youth and uses it for His purposes. When you need a reminder of this, read in Proverbs or think of Joshua, Isaac, Daniel, Gideon, Mary, Jeremiah, Timothy, and David, among others.

Value your adolescence for the joy of the present and for the beauty of its part in the whole scheme of life. Value yourself for yourself.

3. MORNING PRAYER

As you wake up in the morning you feel jumpy, uneasy. You have something to do today and you wonder if you'll make it. The job is too big or too difficult, you can't meet a deadline, or you're hopelessly incapable. What will people think? If only you could have a feeling of confidence in place of a burden or worry.

Well, you're a Christian, so you pray, "Please help me, God." What happens? You go on worrying. Why?

Notice that you're worried because you're depending on yourself. At the same time you think that you're not up to doing the task.

That's the key to your worry and the key to your prayer.

When you pray, forget about yourself and put God at the center of your prayer. Through your prayer give your problem to God ("Cast your burden on the LORD, and he will sustain you," Ps. 55:22a); accept that the outcome will be His will ("And this is the confidence which we have in him, that if we ask anything according to his will he hears us," I John 5:14); desire that whatever you do will glorify Him ("Whatever you ask in my name, I will do it, that the Father may be glorified in the Son," John 14:13); and put all your trust in God to hear and answer your prayer ("And whatever you ask in prayer, you will receive, if you have faith," Matt. 21:22).

Of course you still have to go out and do your part of the job, but you can do it with peace and confidence in God's strength.

4. THE FOREVER FEELING

I will sing of thy steadfast love, O LORD, for ever; with my mouth I will proclaim thy faithfulness to all generations. For thy steadfast love was established for ever, thy faithfulness is firm as the heavens. Psalm 89:1–2

Conditions have to be just right to have *the feeling.*

Your body is in top condition. You're rested. The temperature is neither too hot nor too cold and likely the sun is shining brightly. Your clothes fit so perfectly that they feel as if they belong to your body. Your cares, if you have any, are far in the background and under control. Everything you've done recently has come out just right, or you can hardly wait for something you've planned. There's no place you'd rather be than where you are right now. You wonder how life can be so perfect. You have *the feeling:* you're so happy you think you could jump out of your skin!

"Does this have to end?" you ask yourself. "I wish it could last forever."

And all of a sudden it hits you. That's it!

"I'm going to live forever!" you practically shout. "I'm going to live in heaven—forever. Perfect. Complete joy. Like this, only better. Better than anything I've ever experienced or can possibly imagine. Thank you, Lord!"

The Lord has made everything add up to *the feeling.* Heaven has already begun, even though your experiencing it will have slight interruptions through the rest of your life. But at this moment you know that because Jesus made it possible, you will live forever, in perfect God-praising happiness.

5. TEEN-AGERS ARE GREAT

Rejoice . . . in your youth, and let your heart cheer you in the days of your youth. . . . Ecclesiastes 11:9

Isn't growing up and becoming a teen-ager a great experience? You're becoming stronger physically, finding more abilities in yourself, gaining new freedoms, developing thinking power, and doing more things than you could when you were younger.

Striving, dreaming, planning, and preparing for your future are exciting. Each new experience and discovery spurs you on to the next.

Teen-agers, especially Christian teens, are great. I admire their energy, enthusiasm, and sincerity.

Teens use their energy for sports, recreation, and "messing around," but they also put loads of energy into studying, school activities, and work. Teens are good workers, willing to take jobs for needed pay, but also willing to donate large amounts of time and energy as volunteers who help other people.

Teens can turn almost any activity into a good time. They are also idealistic and want to make the world a better place as well as to improve themselves. When they back a project they can be counted on to get it done.

Most teen-agers are serious, concerned, kind, and polite. They want to do things right and be acceptable not only to their friends but also to everyone. They care about people of all ages.

Today's teen-agers get lots of bad publicity. Newscasts and television movies picture teens as troubled and troublesome. It's unfair to the majority of kids who are normal, admirable, and lovable as you, reader, undoubtedly are.

Thank God for this time of your life.

6. ACCEPT YOURSELF

READ: Matthew 6:25–34.

One of my memories of my teens is that I could be quite unhappy with myself. I desperately wished to make personal improvements and felt like a failure for staying the same.

Then, as now, our culture had standards of an ideal person and sent signals to people of all ages that they'd better reach those standards to be socially acceptable. Of course, many of the ideals were phony or unreasonable. Then, as now, kids would be miserable if they didn't measure up to the teen heroes or other kids.

I wouldn't say that you should stop wishing you were something you are not. Teen-agers are future-oriented, and without some dissatisfaction with the present and striving to be better you would get nowhere in life.

On the other hand, joy is yours when you accept yourself as you are. Excitement is yours when you build your strengths and find new personal attributes.

If you're not good-looking, be kind; if you're not smart, be trustworthy; if you're not popular, be dependable; if you're not a leader, be cheerful; if you're not rich, be helpful; if you're not athletic, be artistic; if you're not the life of the party, cultivate things you like doing alone; if you're here instead of in some more exciting place, find something beautiful here.

If you're not happy all of the time, you're normal, and it doesn't mean that you'll never be happy. But you will be happiest when you like yourself as you are. After all, God loves you as you are.

Pray for the ability to accept yourself.

7. HAPPINESS IN THE BLOOD

READ: I Kings 19.

Teen-age moods often swing from high to low.

Some moods are physically based but temporary; you can recognize and live with them. Circumstances beyond your control can depress you: breaking up with a boyfriend, problems at school, a death in the family. Those times must be endured, but they eventually end.

Moods are not easy to control. It's disgusting when someone says, "Be happy," as if you wouldn't be if you could. It's worse if you are depressed and everyone around you seems happy.

But you can control your response to what's happening and, in turn, the response itself changes your mood. Or you may need to take a break from the depressing situation.

One of my favorite Bible stories is the one about Elijah, when he ran away from Jezebel and became so depressed that he kept on running. It was so human of him.

I think God knew Elijah needed a break, because He let him run far away and had the angel provide food and water. But then God told Elijah to improve his response: he'd acted so depressed he'd convinced himself he wanted to die. God gently chided Elijah for running from his work, assigned him new tasks to build up his feeling of worth, and said to look at the positive side. First, seven thousand men in Israel had not bowed to Baal, so Elijah need not feel so alone and sorry for himself; second, he had simple, everyday blessings at hand—food, water, and the all-important presence of God.

I have a trick that lifts my mood. I say, "I have happiness in my blood," and I will the happiness to start flowing.

Accept your normal mood swings, be as positive as possible, and try to pump some happiness through your veins. And don't forget that God always supports you.

Pray for God's support through your moods.

8. GOOD-LOOKING

READ: the Book of Esther.

We make much of physical beauty. The way we look or think we look helps mold our personalities.

Ten-year-old Chad is extraordinarily handsome, and little else. His good looks preoccupy him and give him confidence. He could be a better athlete, a better student, a better conversationalist, a better leader, and more concerned about other people. Instead he's boring. He makes a good first impression, but kids soon tire of him. His friendships do not last. Chad's beauty is his handicap.

Joan is a woman of elegance. She wears her fashionable clothes with easy assurance. She has a sense of humor, is intelligent, an avid reader, a "with-it" woman. But as a youngster Joan was miserable. She was so shy she seldom spoke up, and dared not make friends because she was sure she was gangly and ugly. As Joan's beauty emerged, she overcame her shyness and was in turn a dancer, a mistress of ceremonies, a fashion model, a public speaker, and a teacher. She still claims that she is shy, but the guests she welcomes to the small resort she and her husband own would never know it. Joan's discovery of her physical beauty unlocked her inner beauty and hidden talents.

Lea, a college senior, is nearly ideal. She has a clever sense of humor, her interests and reading are wide-ranging, she seeks new experiences and converses intelligently on any subject. Unself-consciously poised and kind, she puts everyone she meets at ease. With her dark-haired, dark-eyed natural beauty assured, she has concentrated on other things. Lea's beauty is her support.

The Bible is full of stories of how physical appearance affects relationships with God and people. Beauty, or lack of it, can lead to either good or evil—serving God or self.

Pray for a beauty that reflects the beauty and the love of God.

9. POPULAR

He who is greatest among you shall be your servant. Matthew 23:11

"What I want more than anything else right now is to be popular," is the secret, and sometimes not-so-secret, wish of many teen-agers.

The word *popular* means different things for different teens. Popular persons may act confident, talk easily about themselves, be at the center of attention by entertaining or joking, belong to a certain crowd, have smart mouths, be partygoers, show they have money, be bold or daring, use their talents conspicuously, or merely be perceived by others as being popular.

A girl who is popular has the boys' attention either because of her sparkling personality or, more likely, because of her good looks. A boy is popular who talks easily with girls and has them vying for his attention because of his looks or personality, but more likely because he is a good athlete. A popular person may have followers of the same sex who try to get his or her attention and approval, is "cool" (interpreted for me by one boy as meaning that everyone is afraid of you), or is a hardworking leader who inspires others to get jobs done. Some kids are popular without realizing it themselves, and some think themselves to be popular while no one else does.

The Christian recognizes the ingredients of most of these definitions of popularity to be self-centered and self-serving. But there is another type of personal popularity that is more pleasing to people and to God. It is the popularity of someone who is kind, serves other people and brings out the best in them. That's popularity every Christian can and should have.

Pray for a balanced desire for popularity, based on Christian standards.

10. CLARENCE KLUTZ

READ: James 2:1–17.

It had started toward the end of sixth grade. No one knew where Clarence Clede's family had lived before moving into Old Lady Clede's shabby house on the edge of the village.

Clarence wasn't exactly ugly, but his size was outstanding. "Does that little kid belong in sixth grade?" the class athlete said loudly when the teacher introduced him. "Hey, he's smaller than I am," added short Pete. Clarence didn't respond.

That day the kids went about their activities as if Clarence weren't there. They'd grown up together and weren't used to welcoming strangers.

Toward the end of the afternoon the class was working on its social-studies projects. The teacher had assigned Clarence to the group making a mural. He didn't join in because he didn't know what to do. As he stepped back out of someone's way, he knocked over a jar of poster paint he hadn't seen. "What a klutz!" From then on he was known as Little Clarence Klutz. Kids would purposely set things so he'd knock them over. Then they'd jeer. He became so uptight that he became a genuine klutz.

Through the years Clarence remained on the outside, quietly doing as he was told. He was always chosen last for teams. On the playground he hung around the fence or played with his little sister. Kids remarked about him as if he weren't there or couldn't hear. Or they ignored him.

Finally their hectic senior year ended at graduation. Through it all Clarence had remained silent and practically unseen. Then, as Clarence walked across the stage to receive his diploma, the class gave him one final recognition. "Yea, Klutz, Klutz, Klutz!" they yelled, and mockingly applauded.

No one in the community ever knew what became of Clarence Clede. No one ever thought about the torment of his school years or its lifelong effect on him. No one ever cared.

Repent if you have been unkind to one of God's children.

11. TRIPLE TRAGEDY

READ: Galatians 6:1–10.

There's a little bit of Clarence Klutz in all of us, and a lot in some of us.

Teen-agers fear nothing so much as being slightly different from the rest of the crowd. We try to cover up or make up for our differences.

This explains many of our cruel remarks to or about other kids. By bringing attention to someone else's problem we may look better by comparison; we feel superior if he looks inferior. Or we are part of the "in" crowd as long as we are not with the "outsider." We can join the insiders, or at least get their approval, if we make fun of the outsider.

The obvious tragedy is Clarence Klutz's suffering from this torment. But a deeper tragedy for him is that we prevent him from becoming the potentially loving person he was created to be. When we emphasize only his flaws or differences—as if he has no good points—those flaws are all he eventually sees in himself. He may become shy, withdrawn, afraid to reach out to people. Withdrawal becomes a habit and finally a part of his personality. He cannot love.

But we, too, are victims of this tragedy, for we prevent ourselves from being the loving persons we were created to be. We miss the joy and the satisfaction of reaching out to a human being who needs our love, and the added satisfaction of having the courage to reach out to an "outsider." Instead, we develop the habit of striking out and may end up having to defend ourselves.

Finally, God suffers when we hurt one of His children. The worst tragedy would be if Clarence Klutz's misery stood in the way of his having a loving relationship with God.

Everyone is the loser when we substitute cruelty for love.

Ask God to teach you to love your neighbor.

12. CHRISTIAN PERSONALITY (1)

READ: Ephesians 4:17–5:2.

A group of young Christian adults had turned to serious conversation. "Is there such a thing as a Christian personality?" Bill asked.

"Definitely," Marti responded immediately. "A Christian person is someone who puts others ahead of himself or herself. Kind. Considerate. Gentle."

Marti met many different people in her office. "Not all people with a Christian personality are Christians," she went on, "and not all Christians have a Christian personality. But Christians in general are helpful and pleasant."

"I agree," said Jon, a college freshman. "I think of a Christian as someone you can depend on, who knows how you would feel if he let you down."

"A Christian personality is peaceful, settled, not threatening to anybody," said Rick.

"Treats people with respect. Listens to them. Gets the best out of them," Marti added.

"Yes," said Rick. "I think of a Christian person as being like a kid I knew in high school. He put everyone at ease. In sports or in class he'd encourage kids, and they liked him. Everyone knew he was a Christian, but he never went around announcing it."

Now Anne spoke up. "Everyone is basically different, including Christians. You can't say there's one uniform personality for Christians. It's humanly impossible."

"Granted. And you have to work at having a Christian personality," Marti said. "But the Bible definitely describes Christian personality traits when it talks about the fruit of the Spirit. And it says you have to try to be patient and kind and forgiving and all the rest."

"Obviously we're talking about an ideal," said Jon. "I think above all, a Christian personality should turn people on for the Lord, not against Him."

Pray for guidance in developing your personality.

13. CHRISTIAN PERSONALITY (2)

READ: Colossians 3:1–17.

"You've merely been talking about *nice* people," said Anne. "Many Christians I know aren't so well-liked. They're a bunch of hypocrites and goody-goodies. Preachy."

"Would you say someone with a Christian personality always does the right thing?" Bill asked.

"Maybe tries to," said Anne, "at least what *he* thinks is right."

"The Christian guys in my dorm do what they think is right, but they are quiet and comfortable about it," said Jon. "They're not judgmental, and the other guys respect them."

Sarah had been listening. Now she said, "Why did you ask, Bill?"

"There's this supervisor at work who claims to be a Christian because he goes to church and follows certain rules. But he's so unreasonable, always yelling at people or acting like a big shot. He's an example of what a Christian personality is *not*. I figure I should be able to say what it *is*."

"The Bible tells what a Christian personality should not be when it says to put off certain behavior, like coveting and lying and all that," said Marti. "Paul's writings are full of descriptions of the ideal Christian personality. Mostly it has to do with love."

"Christians can't be perfect," said Sarah, "but I expect them to have something of a Christian personality. It's better publicity for Jesus than being the opposite."

Anne nodded. "I guess if people are changed by the love of Christ their personalities should reflect it. They'll want to share Christ's love. I'll admit there's such a thing as a Christian personality to *strive* for."

With this everyone agreed.

Pray for the opportunity to witness for Christ by being your Christian self.

14. WHAT IS A DAD? (1)

READ: Luke 11:1–13.

A dad is someone who
   is serious about the responsibilities of being a father.
   has a voice that is stronger and more fearsome but also
      more reassuring than your mother's.
   teaches you life's important ideas and principles to live by.
   knows your feelings and needs.
   is your security and protection from the rest of the world.
   will never knowingly do anything to you that's scary or
      harmful.
   is trustworthy.
   makes you feel important when he pays attention to you,
      so you want to do your best for him.
"My dad isn't that perfect," you may say. "Sounds like God."
   True, no dad is perfect and most are far from ideal. Many
fathers have such deep problems that they can't be dads at all.
The Bible calls God our father to explain our love relationship
with Him. The example doesn't work too well if your experience with your father has been unhappy, if he has not
reflected God's love.
   However, this piece is for boys who will someday become
dads. If your dad has not been ideal, you've missed many joys
and satisfactions that you may have to seek elsewhere. If your
dad has not been a good model, you need a substitute. Whatever your past experience, you in turn will be a model for your
own children. The Christian person you are growing to be, your
present models, your fantasizing about your future, are already
molding you into the Christian father you will be.
   And remember, your best model is God.

Thank God for being your father and model.

15. WHAT IS A DAD? (2)

READ: Psalm 103.

The little boy caught up to his dad at the curbside, reached for his hand, and held tightly until they were across the road.
"You help me, Daddy," he said.

The toddler was playing in the sandbox around the corner of the garage. Her father's head was buried under the hood of his car parked in the drive. Their conversation was a singsong exchange: "Dad-dee," "Pam-mee," "Dad-dee," "Pam-mee."

The little auburn-haired girl was the same height as the patient old Irish setter she hugged and petted. Her father stood next to her watching the meeting that had interrupted their evening walk.
"Where will he go?" she asked. "Does he have a daddy?"

When the little children become restless in church, the young fathers, strong and gentle, take them on their laps to calm them. They share these responsibilities with the mothers.

Jim adored his two boys. He'd often give them a pat and a "you're okay" smile. One Sunday Ruth's nephew was in church with them. Jim reached behind Ruth, touched the boy's shoulder, leaned forward and gave him a "you're okay" smile. Jim knew his nephew needed to feel loved while his parents were away.

One warm August evening my dad and I were in the big dark back yard watching the northern lights. The sky was brilliant with flashing lights of all colors. It was too terrible to see and too beautiful to miss. I put my hand in my dad's. With him I was safe on such a scary night. He talked about the wonders of the universe and God the creator. His knowledge and attitudes about nature and God are now mine.

Pray for God's guidance for your own father and for yourself as a future father.

16. BE PATIENT

"I can't wait until dinner's ready."

"Will Friday night ever come?"

"Be patient!" your mother says. You know she's telling you to "calmly tolerate delay while waiting for the right moment." But when you read the words *patient* and *patience* in the Bible you know they have many meanings that describe Christian virtues.

Waiting in prayer. "Trust in the LORD, and do good. . . . Take delight in the LORD, and he will give you the desires of your heart. Be still before the LORD, and wait patiently for him . . ." (Ps. 37:3, 4, 7).

Love. "Love is patient and kind . . ." (I Cor. 13:4).

Humility. ". . . the patient in spirit is better than the proud in spirit" (Eccles. 7:8).

Persevering in God's work. "And as for that [seed] in the good soil, they are those who, hearing the word, hold it fast in an honest and good heart, and bring forth fruit with patience" (Luke 8:15).

Self-control when being provoked or attacked. ". . . we rejoice in our sufferings, knowing that suffering produces endurance, and endurance produces character, and character produces hope, and hope does not disappoint us . . ." (Rom. 5:3–5).

Acceptance of unpleasant persons and slow learners. ". . . admonish the idlers, encourage the fainthearted, help the weak, be patient with them all" (I Thess. 5:14).

Peacemaker. "And the Lord's servant must not be quarrelsome but kindly to every one, an apt teacher, forbearing, correcting his opponents with gentleness" (II Tim. 2:24–25a).

Bearing problems without complaint. "As an example of suffering and patience, brethren, take the prophets. . . . You have heard of the steadfastness of Job, and you have seen the purpose of the Lord, how the Lord is compassionate and merciful" (James 5:10–11).

Pray for patience with all persons in all situations.

17. GETTING ATTENTION

READ: Ephesians 5:15–17.

The young man running the beach concession was busy all day making hamburgers, selling pop and candy, and renting out the rowboats and canoes lined up at the far end of the beach.

In the evening, when business slowed, he had time for friendly chatter and especially enjoyed making the out-of-state campers feel welcome. After he shut down the grill and cleaned up, he made sure the boats were safely on shore, the canoes turned over. Twelve hours made a long day.

One cool evening four girls had been hanging around the nearly deserted beach trying to get the young man's attention. Just as he was putting his broom away he heard a clatter outside. He ran to investigate. He was responsible for the place.

As he got outside he saw a couple canoes begin to drift away from shore. Three of the rowboats were partly in the water. The four girls were laughing as they overturned more boats.

The young man yelled and sloshed into the water to rescue the canoes and the rowboats. He did not have kind words for the girls as they giggled over his plight. "You don't act like you're from around here," he said. "People here take good care of things." He was tired, and he found they'd dislodged even more boats. He was angry as he secured the boats.

It was a crude thing for the girls to do, an immature way to get the young man's attention. As it turned out, it was not at all the kind of attention they'd hoped for.

Sometimes we have such strong urges to get or have attention that we end up making fools of ourselves, or worse, being unkind. In the long run, being friendly in a kindly way is the easier way, and makes the lasting impression we wish to leave on people.

Pray for wisdom for your actions.

18. DRESS CODE

READ: Romans 12:1–2.

Does your school have a dress code? Ours does, but our town doesn't.

The first warm day of spring brought out some startling costumes.

I use the word *costumes* because what we wear is usually intended to convey a message about ourselves, such as: this is my occupation; I'm rich; I know the latest fashions; this is my age; I have a sense of humor; I'm careless; I'm poor; I'm cool; I'm an original; I'm like the rest of you; please notice me; please don't notice me.

That spring day the messages in clothes were: it's a warm day; I'm keeping cool; please notice my body; I'm in college. However, people in the bank, the phone center, and the pediatrician's office weren't too impressed, since their interests were on their phone bills, money, and children's health.

Teen-agers want their clothes to state their individuality while they are accepted by other kids. Teens are usually blind followers of some vague "they"—the trendsetters.

But following a trend can be tricky if you don't know the trendsetters' intended message. Or your intentions can be misunderstood. You may only be saying, "It's warm weather," or, "I'd rather be comfortable than dressed up," or, "My good jacket is in the laundry," while the viewer thinks you sell sex or do grubby work or are a "tough" from the wrong side of town.

Question dress codes that are obviously someone's meaningless exercise of power. Be sure your personal dress code is not a blind imitation of a style whose message you'd rather not send.

Why not wear clothes that send a positive message about yourself?

Ask God to help you make a good impression in His name.

19. SELF-CONSCIOUS

READ: I Peter 4:7–11.

I used to think that when I grew up all my problems would disappear. It hasn't quite turned out that way.

For example, I still have bouts of self-consciousness. I worry about the impression I make on other people. I'm shy and wonder how I look, if I sound okay.

Lately it seems I've been in groups where everyone is self-confident. This makes me feel worse.

I tell myself I'm unfair to me when I compare myself with others; I am what God made me to be and as acceptable as anyone. I don't listen to myself, though.

Self-consciousness can work against us if because of it we value ourselves less than we should or become socially withdrawn. But it can serve a good purpose if the pain of it and the effort to get rid of it drives us to positive resolutions.

I've been working on a solution to my self-consciousness—a solution that should prevent my having it in the first place. I forget about myself and concentrate on other people. I listen to them and care about them—and often find that most people are no more confident than I am. So I try to make them feel comfortable and acceptable to me or to the group. The result is that I'm more pleasant and feel I'm a more worthwhile person.

My prayer is that the beauty of Jesus will be seen in me.

20. DO ADULTS HAVE PROBLEMS?

READ: Romans 12:9–21.

All adults have problems. Possibly your parents or the parents of someone you know have serious problems that affect their children.

What can you do about it? Certainly children your age are not responsible for taking care of their parents or solving their problems. They can only live with the problems as easily as possible.

A first step to living with your parents' problems is understanding them. A second is responding to them lovingly. Most importantly, do not blame yourself for your parents' problems.

Parents are human, with human needs and disappointments: needs for love and recognition that may never have been completely satisfied; disappointments because their dreams about adulthood, marriage, children, and jobs have not worked out.

Parents have a wide range of personalities. They can be inconsistent, unpredictable, and moody, or loving, wise, and fair.

Some parents honestly don't know what their kids need, or what bothers them. If your parents have such deep-seated problems that they actually harm you, you must seek help from someone outside your family whom you trust and respect.

The command to "honor thy father and mother" does not give your parents license to abuse you. It does mean that their humanity demands the same respect, love, and understanding that any human being deserves.

Parents need understanding friends; maybe your parents' friend can be you. Your understanding will lead to tolerance, and tolerance to love.

Pray for the ability to love and understand your parents.

21. WHAT TO EXPECT
OF CHRISTIAN PARENTS

READ: Ephesians 6:1–4.

But, you may ask, what about my parents? They are Christians. Aren't they supposed to be different?

Christian parents are human and have problems, too. But because their hearts have been changed by Jesus' love for them and their love for Jesus, they are assured that the Holy Spirit will help them to be loving and understanding persons. As Christian parents, they have the desire and have made the commitment to God that they will pass on their love and knowledge of Christ to you.

Their ideas of Christian parenthood mean you can expect certain things of them: they will be trustworthy, will not physically harm you, will not allow you to harm them or anyone else, will be patient through your trying moods, will listen and try to see your point of view. They should not spoil you by making you think that you are more important than you really are.

Expect your parents to teach you a Christian way of life. They will love you for being the unique human being you are. And they will discipline you, train you, and keep you within the bounds of loving and safe behavior. Above all, you can expect your Christian parents to support you with their prayers.

It was in God's loving plan for you that you should be born to your particular set of parents. His expectations of them are spelled out in the Bible. But He knows they are not perfect or problem-free, and neither should you expect them to be.

Pray for God's guidance for your parents.

22. FORGIVE

READ: Ezekiel 18.

"Well, all fine and good," you may say, "but my parents and I still fight. I'm sick and tired of taking all the blame for everything that goes wrong. Besides, there's no hope that my parents will change for the good."

Blame is tricky to deal with. It's often a form of "buck-passing" that makes an unpleasant situation worse. In any controversy, family or otherwise, blame is seldom all on one side.

True, the Bible places much responsibility on parents for their influence on their children, for being models for their children to imitate. It says that the sins of the fathers follow to the "third and fourth generations." You can see it in the ways your parents are like your grandparents. As you get older you will more and more recognize your parents in yourself. You can't entirely escape being in your parents' mold, with exceptions.

First, you are ultimately responsible for what you are and what you do. The older you get the more responsible you are for yourself.

Second, you can change yourself for the better. Even though basic personality traits may be inherited or learned from your parents, you can and must make the effort to change when necessary. Change comes through belonging to Christ, the power of prayer, and help from the Holy Spirit.

Finally, you must forgive your parents for ways they have failed you or mistakes they have made. Your understanding of them leads to forgiveness. Forgiveness goes far toward eliminating the problem. Forgiveness restores love.

Forgiveness is Christ's way.

Pray for the ability to forgive your parents' errors.

23. WATCH THAT TONE OF VOICE

A soft answer turns away wrath, but a harsh word stirs up anger.
Proverbs 15:1

Teachers of composition tell students to pay attention to their tone of voice. That's more difficult in writing than in speaking. Yet, when the printed words are read aloud the tone of voice becomes apparent.

Tone of voice communicates the attitude of the writer or the speaker, and gets a certain response from the reader or the listener.

Tone of voice is something we seldom plan, yet it is easily controlled. For example, the less we know a person, the more we control our tone of voice when talking with him or her.

Often, particularly with members of our family, a sassy or angry tone of voice is a habit or an unconscious imitation of another member of the family. We don't mean to bawl out each other or make each other feel dumb, but we do so unthinkingly through our tone. Check this by listening to families in stores or restaurants. Parents give their children simple instructions in angry tones, children respond in sassy tones; spouses exchange simple information in derogatory tones, responses are in defensive tones. The results: arguments and hurt feelings.

What about your family? Do some of you use an unintentionally rancorous tone of voice? Check your own tone. Gently ask other unthinking family members, "Are you talking that way because you're mad at me?" Explain how their tone of voice makes you feel.

A final hint. If a conversation becomes really heated, don't respond until things have cooled down. Then calmly discuss your point and your tone of voice: "Mom, it hurts me when we sound like. . . ."

A controlled tone of voice works wonders in keeping the peace.

Pray for a loving tone in your family communication.

24. THROUGH THEIR EYES

READ: Matthew 12:46–50.

Put yourself in your parents' place and try to see yourself through their eyes.

Once you were a baby—cute, cuddly, innocent, fascinating because you were new, precious because you were the product of your parents' love.

You were dependent on them, and everyone has a special love for a being who depends on him or her. You were an extension of them, and as you grew your parents tried to mold you to fit their dreams of what they hoped you would become.

But you didn't remain a cute, dependent, pliable baby. You've steadily grown to be more independent. You have your own ideas and activities, friends and responsibilities, experiences that your parents never had.

Of course your parents know it would be unfair for them to keep you dependent and doing only their will. They know that you must learn to go out into the world to do your own Christian service. But it's hard on them. You are a reminder that they are getting older and that they must release control of you.

And, naturally, you've not turned out to be the dream person your parents expected of their little baby. You've become yourself, and for your parents that can be quite startling or disappointing or embarrassing. So be patient with them when they don't quite know how to respond to you or when that causes them, in turn, to embarrass you. (However, you really give your parents more reason to be proud than disappointed.)

God made no mistake in matching you with your parents. Cherish them for the good things they have done for you.

Pray that your growing up will be a happy experience for your parents.

25. THEY'RE ALWAYS MAKING ME GO TO CHURCH

I was glad when they said to me, "Let us go to the house of the LORD!" Psalm 122:1

So you and your family attend church regularly and always have. Either you have an unusually exciting church or you are a very mature Christian if you have never thought: church is boring, tiring, depressing; I don't understand the minister; I'm too weary, busy, interested in other things; it's too warm, too cold, too nice outside; I should make my own decision about going to church; I shouldn't be here if I don't like it or just daydream.

All Christians have such thoughts at some time or other, thoughts that need not make you feel guilty. However, here are some ways you can help your church attendance be a more positive experience.

Remember that the church service is a time to worship God, talk to Him, hear His Word, express love for other Christians, learn about salvation and its meaning in your life, give gifts to God, confess your sins, and dedicate your life to Him.

Instead of concentrating on the things you dislike, look for something new in each service: a new thought about God, a special moment of praise or thanksgiving, a personal communication with God, something memorable.

Be active. Through your youth group, for example, you may bring about changes in the church service.

Understand that as your parents exercise their authority by forcing you to go to church, they fulfill their responsibility for your spiritual education. Someday, when you are independent, you may look for a different church.

Finally, appreciate your church for having taught you a basic knowledge of and proper response to God. It is a priceless foundation for your life.

Pray for a blessing on your church attendance.

26. WHY CHURCH?

READ: I Timothy 4:11–16.

"But why go to church?" you may ask. "Can't I be a Christian without going to church? I can love God no matter where I am."

True, you can love God in any place, and salvation through Christ does not depend upon regular church attendance. However, being part of the church completes or rounds out the Christian life. That relationship consists of three general areas, distinct but intertwined. To overemphasize one or to neglect one or two is to be a lopsided or partial Christian, to cheat yourself out of many of Christ's blessings.

One area of Christian life is a personal relationship with God: private communication with Him through prayers, Bible study, meditation, His presence in your life, your praise and thanksgiving, and following His will.

Another is the general area of witness. This has to do with your public self, your relationship with the world, where Christ is seen as the dominant factor in your life, where you share His love and bring His healing to a hurting world. It involves your lifestyle and your personality. It may lead to a fulltime profession of Christian service.

And then there is the church, the body of believers, the communion of saints. The church is where Christ's people nurture and support each other, learning through Bible study. In the church you are both giver and recipient. A Christian needs the church's support and should use it as an outlet for his or her Christian expression.

You go through cycles or phases, during which you need one area of the Christian life more than another. But sooner or later you need all three to make your Christian life complete.

Thank God for your church.

27. PARABLE OF THE TREE SEEDS

READ: Ephesians 4:11–16.

During May, certain trees in my neighborhood produce blizzards of seeds that remind me of giant flakes of oatmeal.

The seeds float on the breeze, then drift into corners of steps, walls, and sidewalks, and around grasses and shrubs.

This spring produced an extra-large crop and the seeds became a nuisance. After more-than-normal rainfall, the piles of seeds became soggy and remained stuck in corners. When warm weather followed, something happened I'd not noticed other years. The piles of seeds turned green with tiny two-leaved sprouts. By sticking together the seeds nourished each other. A few in each pile would gain hold in the soil, though they would first have to push through wood or asphalt.

One Sunday I thought, "The seeds are like God's people, blown together by the Holy Spirit, sticking close to nourish each other. Each little pile is like a congregation of Christ's church."

But not all the seeds had stuck together. After a couple weeks many individuals were still finding their way around. Several tracked into the house. I picked a few off the carpet and for the first time really saw them. They were neither round nor symmetrical. They were delicate but perfectly structured for drifting far, penetrating the ground, sprouting, and becoming trees that would someday produce blizzards of their own. No two seeds were identical.

I was reminded that every Christian is unique. Some Christians need the security of a tight group or tradition; some prefer anonymity. Others do better as individuals, going out on their own and finding their own spots to take root.

But all together they form the beauty and the wonder of God's universal church, doing His work and His will.

Thank God for the family of Christ and the place it has for all kinds of individuals.

28. PROMISES

Bill hated to leave the store while two customers waited for his partner to help them. The business couldn't afford to lose customers, but it was already past five and the kids would be waiting.

The heavy traffic irritated Bill. He didn't really have time to coach, but he loved soccer and he loved kids, and the league needed every coach it could get.

"You're late, Bill," the kids shouted as he hurried across the playground. They looked dejected.

"Hi," he said. "Where are Mike and Kenny?"

"They quit. Said they didn't feel like practicing."

"Don't let them play if they don't practice, Coach."

Bill's heart sank. "We need them," he said. "We don't have that many kids. See if you can talk them into coming back."

Just because they didn't feel like practicing? Bill felt hurt for himself and for the team. Mike's and Kenny's signing on was their promise to help, and the team came to depend on them. Now they'd let everyone down. They'd broken a promise.

Why should you keep a promise? A promise is an invitation to someone to depend on you. He entrusts you with the care of part of his well-being. You know how he would feel if you broke your promise.

Keeping a promise is a reflection of Christ. The promises God makes and keeps are for our well-being, so we entrust ourselves to Him. His greatest promise was to rescue us from the punishment for our sins.

Keeping a promise isn't always comfortable, just as it wasn't comfortable for Christ to suffer a horrible death in order to secure our eternal well-being. But His people depended on it, and He kept to the task.

So, you see, keeping a promise is a Christian act.

But I trust in thee, O LORD, I say, "Thou art my God." My times are in thy hand. Psalm 31:14–15a

29. THINGS ARE NOT ALWAYS AS THEY SEEM

Do not judge by appearances. . . . John 7:24

Kenny was unlocking his bike after school as Mike stopped in front of him. "Hi," said Mike. "You going to soccer practice?"

"Yeah, I guess so, but I don't feel like it. Are you?"

"No. I'm quitting the team. I'm tired of being yelled at," Mike answered.

"So am I. Especially from Kevin. Can you just quit?" asked Kenny.

"My dad said I can if I want to. Last time I got home from practice he found out why I wasn't too happy. He said I don't have to take being yelled at, and it's okay with him if I'm no great soccer player."

"Wow! I think I'll quit too," said Kenny. "At least being on the team isn't something we *have* to do, like gym. Anyway, Mr. Norden won't let the kids yell at each other in class. Bill's not so strict."

"I'm going over to the arcade. Do you want to go along?"

"Okay! Sounds better than soccer practice."

As Mike and Kenny rode toward the mall they met a couple of kids from the soccer team.

"Where're you guys going? Aren't you coming to practice?"

"No," said Mike. "We're quitting."

"How come?"

"We don't feel like practicing," said Kenny.

Kenny wasn't lying, but the truth was in what he left unsaid.

It's easy to make judgments based on the way things appear. The reasons for people's behavior can be painful for us to admit. The other members of the team may have been surprised to know that they were responsible for Kenny's and Mike's quitting.

Pray for insight into your effect on other people.

30. THE YELLERS

READ: James 1.

Five boys were at the playground when Kevin arrived. "Here I am, your high-scoring player," he announced. "See what I've got." Kevin was taller than the others, his voice louder.

The boys huddled around him as he produced a box of firecrackers and some matches. "You gonna use them here?"

"Sure. Bill won't be here for a while," Kevin said as he lit a match. The boys ran in all directions, screaming and laughing.

They'd just exploded a whole bundle when Jeff came, grinning as usual. "Hey, here's M 'n' M!" Kevin yelled.

"Yup, here I am, ball hog," Jeff yelled back as he got off his bike. "Watch me connect with this dandelion." He purposely missed and fell down and everyone laughed.

"C'mon," someone said. "Coach told us to start practice while we wait for him."

"Yeah," Kevin shouted, "let's give Jeff some mow-and-miss practice." Everyone laughed, but soon the bitterness of the last game, which they had lost, took over.

"Can't you see twenty yards, stupid? Some dummies don't know how to return a pass."

"Shut up, you're always missing passes. Quit playing for the other team, dumbhead."

"Come on, Fatso, get in position."

"You don't see *me* missing passes." Kevin's sneering voice and self-confidence made his name-calling contagious. The boys joined him as a defense against his derision, while inside they were hurt and nervous. They feared Kevin's influence, but seemed helpless to resist.

Pray for help to resist joining in what you disapprove.

31. THE REMARK THAT STICKS

READ: James 3:6–18.

Most adults would likely agree that some remark made about them during their adolescence hurt so deeply that they never got over it.

Remarks made to kids can shape their lifelong attitudes about themselves. The boy who is called Fatso thinks he is fat, then stays fat through adulthood. The girl whose mistake in math is ridiculed does poorly in math ever after.

Small remarks, whether complimentary or derogatory, remembered or forgotten, affect a person's self-concept. Unfortunately, the American habit is to be critical, mean, angry, to cut each other down rather than to build up.

Why? One often-mentioned reason is our competitiveness. A basic need is to be recognized, honored, loved; in order to build up ourselves we tear down others. It makes us look better by comparison if they look worse. Someone's being worse off than we are puts us a notch higher on our scale of self-worth.

Bad-mouthing is like a disease—contagious. We can be unaware of having the habit. Just as a soccer team can bad-mouth itself out of existence, any group that has the disease suffers.

We have a responsibility to consider the possible effect of what we say, no matter how thoughtless or innocent our motives. While it is not easy to keep from making negative remarks, neither do we have to follow a troublesome leader or an influential crowd.

Pray for reminders not to make careless remarks that will hurt other people.

32. WHERE IS COOL KEVIN COMING FROM?

READ: James 4:11–12.

How was the team to know that Kevin was not happy?

Kevin rarely saw his father, who was obsessed with his thriving business, spending long hours at his office and days out of town. When he did see Kevin, they shared only one interest: sports. "How's my star doing?" his father would ask.

"I'm best on the team. I scored the most goals Saturday."

"That's my son," his father would say. "Keep on winning." And that was all.

Kevin's mother was a beautiful, unsmiling woman who spent much of her time away from home or talking on the phone, "being important," Kevin thought. The only attention she gave Kevin when he was little was to scream about how messy he was. He grew out of that, and now all his mother cared about was his poor grades in school. When her friends came she'd introduce her "handsome son" and laugh too loudly at the silly things he did.

Kevin sensed that his mother favored his older sister, who occupied herself with girlish mysteries and was satisfied when her "stupid little brother" was out of her way.

So Kevin got attention on his own. He practically dragged it out of the other kids. They, not knowing the problems within his family, allowed him to influence them. Many took his cutting remarks to heart and bore them in silence.

Sometimes the people who appear to be cool—leaders, or those we fear and allow to hurt our feelings—are not so strong and confident and well-off as we think. It helps to remember that they, too, need love and understanding.

Pray for understanding of all types of people.

33. CONSIDER THE SOURCE

READ: James 4:1–10.

It would be unfair to think that all kids who act like Kevin have families who are at fault. Often kids who have everything in their favor still feel compelled to act out certain needs, and no one else can make a judgment as to the reason.

However, understanding that the cool kids or the "in" crowd are usually not 100 percent happy or confident helps you to deal with them.

I am not suggesting that you must assume that all kids have hidden personal problems for you to discover and solve. Rather, it's enough to know that all kids have the universal need for love.

Furthermore, you do not have to be put down by what other kids say to you; you do not have to let their problems ruin you.

While some people are consistently cruel or continually trying to make themselves seem important, others are followers or joiners, afraid of being left out. Those who seem to be confident members of certain crowds may actually be insecure people, avoiding the possibility of being scared and lonely, needing each other to impress each other. The walls they build around themselves and their haughtiness about the rest of the world are in reality the protective devices of frightened people.

When you are the object of cruel words or acts, remember they do not necessarily reflect on you as a person. Your understanding of their source will help you ignore them and accept yourself. So much the better if you can help the kids work through their problems.

Pray that you can keep other people's cruel words and acts in perspective.

34. MORAL

READ: Job 31.

Two popular words that label people or their actions are "moral" (good) and "immoral" (bad).

The dictionary's definition of "moral" includes conscience, standards of right and wrong, and being righteous, fair, and honorable. Moral standards may be set by custom or culture.

The moral standards defined in the Bible are set by God. Next to the story of salvation through Christ, morality is the Bible's major theme.

What God in His Word emphasizes as being moral are duty to one's neighbor, completeness, honesty, and human rights. He says to help the helpless, the widow, and the orphan; guarantee the human rights of slaves and strangers; refuse bribes; do not overcharge; feed and clothe the poor; judge fairly; pay employees promptly and fairly; give a full day's work for wages; use no violence.

Then what is "immoral"? It's immoral to use other people, at their expense, to satisfy your greed or desire for pleasure. It's immoral to decrease the quality or the strength of someone else in order to increase your own status or power.

God's moral laws were made to protect people, not to hinder them. They are as modern as they are ancient. They apply to power-grabbing tyrants and land-grabbing nations, to business owners or labor groups overcharging on prices or wages, to adults and children using relatives and acquaintances to build their own feelings of importance.

In short, God's moral standard is the law of love.

Pray for guidance in knowing whether an act is moral or immoral.

35. IMMORALITY—AGAINST GOD

READ: I John 4:13–21.

Love does no wrong to a neighbor; therefore love is the fulfilling of the law. Romans 13:10

If you are thinking that the word *immoral* must cover more than hurting other people, you are right. Immorality is basically an offense against God. But the two are closely connected.

God's reason for making people is so He will have their love, honor, respect, companionship, praise, and glorification. People's most basic need is to totally love Him. God has to have His creatures communicate their love to Him just as He has to communicate His love to them.

God has emotions, from joy to despair. Our withholding our love saddens Him. Rebellion against Him and against the nature of things as He had created them angers Him. Therefore, saddening or angering God is immorality against Him.

Every single person, as a reflection of God, needs to love and be loved. God loves people as deeply as He does because they are His handiwork and they are so much like Him. He has parental love for each of His children, and to hurt or withhold love from one of them is to hurt Him. To hurt one of God's children is to symbolically hurt God, just as someone damaging something you have made hurts you. Therefore, immoral acts against human beings are immoral acts against God.

All immorality is against God, whether it is against Him or against His creatures. The other side is morality: love God, love His children.

Pray that your actions will express your love to God.

36. IMMORALITY—AGAINST YOURSELF

READ: I Corinthians 6:9–20.

Is it possible to be immoral to your own self? Unfortunately, yes. People do many unloving, harmful things to themselves, both physical and spiritual, which break down their integrity, wholeness, quality, and strength. They prevent themselves from being the loving creatures they were meant to be.

A self-indulgence is immoral when it leaves little time, energy, or interest for loving relationships, meeting responsibilities, or appreciating God's gifts.

Being untrue to yourself or your beliefs in order to gain attention or social approval and leaving a false impression of yourself are immoral. To deliberately harm your health or invite physical injury is immoral. Self-enslaving addictions to drugs and alcohol are immoral.

Immoral acts against yourself bring pleasure (usually temporary) at your own expense (usually long-term harmful results).

You may be saying, "But it's my life. If I don't hurt anyone else, how can what I do to myself be immoral?"

Your unloving actions toward yourself are offensive to God, because you are created and loved by Him. He feels your pain and unhappiness. Harming someone He loves (you) is immoral because it is unloving to Him.

For God's sake, and yours, love yourself. That's moral.

Thank God that you belong to Him and that He loves you.

37. THE GOOD FIGHT

READ: Ephesians 6:10–20.

Are you on fire to change the world? Do you look at immorality and injustice and want to convince all people to love God and each other?

Now is the time to get started. Build on your teen-age enthusiasm for making the world a better place for God's sake. Here are some suggestions for doing it effectively.

First, take stock of the present. Start to establish your own convictions about morality. This is no quick and simple exercise, but God's Word will guide you. Measure your own behavior and relationships by your moral standard before you judge others. Start educating yourself for a possible future career in which you can be a force for good.

Second, take action. Learn to reach out to people and to deal with them in all kinds of situations. Volunteer for service projects, or join a group that promotes humanitarian causes or works to eliminate social injustice.

Third, be positive when you fight immorality. Be firm but loving in presenting your convictions. Go to the source of immorality in people's hearts and convince them to change their life philosophies. Do not mistake self-righteousness, political or psychological power, or a forcing of your own lifestyle on other people for true moral reform. Be understanding, tactful, prayerful.

Finally, don't give up. A Christian's work for love and justice to all people is a lifelong love response to God.

Pray for enthusiasm and understanding to correct immorality.

38. IS SEX WICKED?

READ: Genesis 2:18–25 and Titus 1:15.

Is sex wicked?

It is not. It is God's tool for the miraculous procreation of people.

Is it wrong to enjoy sex?

Certainly not. Besides its reproductive purpose, God created it to be a source of joy for men and women and an expression of their Christian love.

Then why are there so many restrictions on it? When is it immoral?

Sex is a powerful instinct. It is immoral when satisfying the instinct leads to exploitation of other persons or to a self-destructive lifestyle.

Since sex leads to the creation of children, God places it within the setting of marriage and family, providing loving and reliable companionship for parents and responsible care of children.

Am I wicked when I think or talk about sex?

No, you're normal.

Why are grownups embarrassed about sex if the Bible isn't?

Mostly because they were brought up to be embarrassed by it.

Why do grownups act silly about sex?

Largely because of embarrassment, or to act bold. Likely that's behind many of the sex jokes on television.

Should I learn about sex?

You can't avoid it. If necessary, urge your parents to find a book that will help your family discuss sex.

Would sex be wicked for me?

Kissing your boyfriend? No. Going all the way with your girlfriend? Yes; you're not married. But you will arrive at that answer yourself if you are informed, consider the results, and are guided by Christian love. Be sure not to exploit or be exploited through sex.

Pray for wisdom and restraint and God's support.

39. READY

READ: Psalm 23.

I had looked to the left, then right, then straight ahead, and started across the highway. The van came up on my left so quickly that I was in front of it before I saw it. The van skidded to the left and my car to the right as we both braked. By fractions of an inch and a second I was spared a violent death.

That was years ago, but the vision of what almost happened still makes me shudder. Even more shocking, I was not so prepared to die as my Christian faith had me think I was. Clearly it was not God's time for me to die, and in the intervening years He's given me many reasons to be alive. But I continue to wonder about my lack of readiness.

I now realize that preparing for death is an experience I don't want to miss. I want time to know my death is approaching. I want to experience breaking with this life, knowing everything is behind me, complete, unchangeable.

I want heaven and eternity to be more desirable and the longing to be with God stronger than any yearning I've ever imagined. I want to have a purer faith than ever before. I want to experience the impact of my salvation in Christ, when I'm past my present distractions.

I admit wanting to avoid pain or a dehumanizing old age. I hope I will not desire death so as to escape an unbearable life. But if that's the Lord's way of preparing me, I want to experience my acceptance and His extra measure of strength.

Death is the inescapable experience. Readiness for death is an experience I hope I won't miss.

Getting ready to die has nothing to do with age. It begins now.

Thank God that your life and death are in His hands.

40. NATURE LOVERS

READ: Psalm 104.

Nature inspires us to praise the glory of God.

From the occasional park visitor to the serious gardener, from the shoreline fisherman with a can of worms to the sophisticated photographer of exotic animals, from the small child wondering about a butterfly to the cellular biologist doing cancer research—almost everyone finds in nature beauty, security, or miracle.

Human life depends on all parts of nature. Although it is violent and unpredictable, people now better understand and control nature more than ever before. With less fear of nature than our ancestors had, we appreciate its beauty. Growing threats to the environment make nature even more precious.

Why do people love nature?

For many it is romantic. Nature is the setting of stories, the place to which city people escape, where busy people relax and families make pleasant memories.

In nature we find dependability in its patterns and laws, surprise in its contrasts and irregularities, fascination with its cause and effect, wonder over each new discovery.

We are drawn to living things because we are living. In them we see part of the miracle of our own being.

A friend once told me that love of nature is religious. That sounded pagan; we don't worship nature. But he is right. A Christian's love of nature is tied to a love for God. In nature we are close to His presence. Nature is God's creation, a result of His divine plan. Our life in common with all living things symbolizes God's plan for us, for eternity.

To love nature, to love life, is to love God. And to praise Him.

Praise God for His beauty that He shows us in nature.

41. THUNDERSTORM

READ: Revelation 21:1–4.

My moods are very responsive to the weather: up with sunshine, down with steady rain, depressed by clouds, frightened by deep cold, excited by thunderstorms.

To me, spring doesn't begin until we've had a good thunderstorm, and summer's height of excitement is when a long hot spell breaks in a slam-bang storm.

Just before the storm you know something big is in the air. The best thunderstorm comes slowly from the distance. All outdoors waits breathlessly as the distant rumble comes closer and the pale flashes of light become brighter. A restless breeze rustles through the trees, as if they are sucking in their breath to brace against the coming fury. A few drops fall, there is a loud crack nearby, and suddenly the wind and the rain hit in earnest. As the rain continues you think about the dry thirsty ground and all the plants getting a good drink.

Then comes the beautiful morning after the storm—clear, cool, sunny, all nature's colors paintbox bright. And, oh, do you feel good—clean, dry, lightweight, strong, capable, tuned-in.

Storms and their aftermath are like life. A storm can destroy human life and property, even while it is exciting. But the calm and the beauty that almost always follow the storm complete it.

God uses contrast and variety in people's lives as well as in nature. You may see only fear and destruction in the stormy times, or you may find in them challenge and excitement or the power and beauty of God. But in the calm and loveliness that follow the stormy times you find relief and joy and praise.

Praise God for the promise He keeps to turn our sorrows into praise.

42. OH, WHAT A BEAUTIFUL MORNING

READ: Psalm 33.

This morning I argued with myself. God was the winner.

It was the most beautiful morning we'd had the whole month of May—clear, cool, and washed clean following a hot, humid, rainless spell.

One part of me said I should discipline myself to stay inside and get my work done, that I had a deadline with people counting on me. The other part said, "I've not been outdoors on a Wednesday morning in May since I was five years old. It will be a whole year before we have another May morning like this. I should really get out walking so I can appreciate it."

I took the walk.

The week before, I'd walked that same route and thought I'd seen all the season's tree blossoms, but this morning I was amazed to see things I'd never seen before—light green blossoms on hardwoods, white blossoms on chokecherries and fragrant locusts, trees that had blossomed the week before now in full summer foliage—all against a brilliant blue sky.

As I neared home I realized I'd walked practically the whole way looking up, actually and symbolically.

The brilliant surroundings, the thrill of discovery, the joy of health—the whole experience put me in touch with God and set me to overflowing with praise. I was sure God had set up the whole neighborhood and the bright morning just so I would absorb the experience and praise Him for it. No other task I'd set for myself could be so important as my walk of praise.

As I said, God was the winner of my argument with myself.

Pray that you will take the opportunities God gives you to praise Him.

43. ALONE ON THE BEACH

READ: I Chronicles 16:23–34.

I thought the sunset might be spectacular that early June evening as I drove out to the state park. But a cloud bank with a few small breaks moved in and soon cast a gray haze over everything.

The rarely-calm water of Lake Michigan was smooth to infinity, banded with subtle pale shades of gray, silver, and green. As I walked far down the lonely stretch of beach between the water's edge and the sand dunes, only three people appeared in the dusk, and they soon disappeared. I was glad, for the hugeness of the lake and sky and beach seemed to stretch even further when void of people; yet the muffling haze created an intimacy and a friendliness far different from the usual excitement of wind and breakers.

Gradually I realized how totally alone I was. I stopped and faced the water, and cherished the feeling of aloneness that overwhelmed me. But even stronger was God's nearness, and His presence filled the vastness of the place. I heard myself say, as to a near and dear friend, "Oh, God, I love you."

My meditation was interrupted by little flashes of silver in the calm water a couple feet from shore—tiny fish reminding me that almost every square inch of the earth contains living creatures to keep us company.

The light was almost gone when I returned to my car. As I drove away my intimacy with God lingered. It had been an hour in which my extreme aloneness had also been a time of intense nearness to God.

Seek the LORD and his strength, seek his presence continually!
I Chronicles 16:11

44. A TOUCH OF TIME

READ: Psalm 90 and Ephesians 1:3–10.

"Pieces of pottery are man's oldest artifacts," the potter said as he handed me a pot from his collection. "They put me in a tradition that reaches back to earliest times. I can pick up a pot and put my fingers in the fingerprints of the person who made it maybe thousands of years ago. It is uniquely shaped to his hand and I can hold it in mine, almost as if it is his physical remains. That's a moving experience."

I pick up a pebble and look at its buff-colored honeycomb-like patterns. Once corals lived in the ancient seas that covered this land on which we stand. Each chamber contained, millions of years ago, a living being that left its skeleton in this now-fossilized colony.

I am part of time, and as I touch time's remains, I think of God and eternity. As I put myself in touch with the potter of long ago and am part of the stream of man's time, or as I put myself in touch with the fossil and am part of the earth's time, or as I contemplate the stars and am part of space time, I know my God, the creator, is greater than anything my human mind can comprehend.

The psalmist was awed when he looked at the stars, though he knew little about space and nothing of speed of light and light years. Today's Christian has so much more knowledge of creation, which inspires awe of the creator.

"With God, all things are possible." The possibilities in creation are beyond human understanding and measurement. "He chose us in him before the foundation of the world." The God of time beyond comprehension is the God of eternity.

Pray that you will not limit your faith in God to what you can comprehend.

45. MANMADE BEAUTY

READ: Psalm 8.

An old-world custom is congratulating the parents for their children's achievements. I did that once in New York City.

The evening rush hour was winding down after a perfect, clear, sunny July day that I'd spent on a bus tour of Manhattan. New York was as great as I'd expected it to be. The final stop was the Empire State Building.

As I stepped onto the observation deck, I was stunned by the sight. Stretching as far as the eye could see was a continuous pattern of upright blocks—skyscrapers and other buildings made uniform by their common reflection of the rosy-gold setting sun, contrasted with the pale blue sky and patches of river, park, and ocean. From that height life's roar was hushed and all suffering and ugliness hidden by the golden roofs and walls. The city was the sum of its millions of people and billions of parts, an organism made by people for people, more beautiful than a photograph or the imagination could ever capture.

I congratulated its Parent. "God! What a creature You have made to be able to do *this!*"

Manmade beauty can be as exciting as nature's beauty for its pattern, color, rhythm, contrasts, shapes, expected regularity, and surprising variety. People's cleverness, inventiveness, skill, and hard work produce the awesome beauty of a bridge, a dam, a miniature carving, a piece of music or literature. "God, what a creature You have made!"

Children are an extension and a reflection of their parents, bringing pride to the parents when they do something good or beautiful. People are an extension and a reflection of God. The good and beautiful things they do bring praise to His glory.

Praise God as the source of all that is clever and artistic in people.

46. HIGH ON HEALTH

READ: I Corinthians 3:16–17.

Want a high without using drugs? Try good health and vigorous exercise. You may have to work up to it, but it's available for free.

Here's a starter. Wake up after a good night's sleep, become aware of your body, and think, "Hey, everything is still working!" The miracle of your complex body-systems continuously functioning is astounding. Praise God!

Next, have a positive attitude toward your health. Don't concentrate on your imperfections. They are likely mere irritants, not life-or-death problems.

Believe what you read and hear about the value of exercise and sensible eating. Both make you feel terrific. Take advantage of your school's physical-education program, which teaches you lifelong personal sports and exercise habits. Then start your own program of exercise, rest, and nutritious eating. The better condition you're in, the better you will feel in general.

Now you are ready for the real high that follows vigorous exercise. A study of runners, who claim a high better than one induced by drugs, confirmed that exercise does indeed cause the body to produce a feeling of euphoria. If drugs are a temptation, physical fitness and exercise are your alternatives.

True, physical afflictions may draw Christians close to God, but I believe that for ordinary day-by-day living, good health and the resulting sense of well-being enhance a praise relationship with God.

And the euphoria following vigorous exercise brings special praise to God. At that moment you know your body is the temple of the Holy Spirit.

It is life's ultimate high.

Pray for good health with which to praise God.

47. MOST BEAUTIFUL

Then God said, "Let us make man in our image, after our likeness. . . ." Genesis 1:26

Remember when you were a little kid and the words *naked* and *bare* ("the table was bare," or "the naked truth") set you squirming and giggling?

Why? Because you immediately thought about the human body, and the idea of it being naked or bare embarrassed you.

Is any particular part of the human body really nasty, silly, embarrassing, or wicked? Or why, at any rate, do we think so?

Our attitudes toward our bodies have been taught us largely by our parents, culture, or other kids. When we were very small we had no idea that any part of the body is embarrassing. But other people gave us the idea that certain areas (those pertaining to sex and elimination) are nasty.

But isn't it true that certain parts of the body should be covered? And isn't there such a thing as a really dirty picture, for instance? Yes, because people exploit each other or indulge their own feelings by turning what is beautiful and natural into a perverse pleasure. No particular part of the body is bad; it's what people make of it.

When God created people He made no mistakes. All parts of the human body are necessary to the other parts, functioning as a whole. Every complex part is a miracle of being, beautiful, a result of the divine plan that pleased God when He created it.

We are more comfortable keeping some parts of our bodies private, and it is our right to keep them private and protected. But out of respect for what God has created, we must not be ashamed of any parts of our bodies.

Glorify God for the human being—the most beautiful and precious part of His creation.

And God saw everything that he had made, and behold, it was very good. Genesis 1:31

48. HOLOCAUST

READ: Isaiah 40:12–31.

Holocaust! Nuclear war! Megadeath, suffering, destruction. No place on earth safe from the fallout. Unimaginable, but possible.

With the buildup of nuclear weapons, worldwide peace movements and anti-nuclear sentiments are growing. But no one is sure a nuclear war—either a single explosion or world wide holocaust—will not happen.

And the thought that a nuclear war would destroy all forms of life on this planet is unbearable, because man has a basic need to know that a part of him and some form of life as he knows it will live after he dies.

But who can say how the world will end? Some scriptural prophesies read like scenarios of nuclear destruction; many do not.

What can we do? Christians are right to be in the forefront of a peace movement; Christianity *is* a peace movement. It begins with person-to-person love and moves out to eliminate all injustice and inhumane action. It transforms people's hearts through the love of Jesus.

God never promises that Christians will not be caught up in the results of the world's evils. And I cannot tell you not to be afraid. No one can help fearing horror such as a nuclear holocaust. Is there any comfort?

Yes, God promises to support His people through all horror and suffering. He does not want them to be paralyzed by fear. Prayer, faith, and action change things—and strengthen us.

Pray for God's peace in the world and for your own peace of mind.

49. HABAKKUK AND THE HOLOCAUST

. . . the righteous shall live by his faith. Habakkuk 2:4

Habakkuk? Who ever reads that book of the Bible? No one I know of. Not I, I thought as my eye fell on the title page. The man was a very minor prophet indeed. What does he have to say?

Plenty, I found out as I began reading. By substituting a few words I could imagine he was writing today. Habakkuk was depressed by the same things that upset today's preachers: violence, crime, unfairness, pride, greed, people taking advantage of each other.

Besides, God tells Habakkuk that, instead of answering his prayers to make things better, He will let things get worse. The worst, most frightening manmade destruction the world has known will come over Habakkuk's homeland. Judah's holocaust is on the way in the form of the Chaldean invaders.

As I read the Book of Habakkuk I noticed how the language describing the Chaldean threat and its results resembles that describing nuclear holocaust, to the point where even survival would be horrible.

Habakkuk's reaction is normal: he's scared and he thinks it's unfair that the good and innocent people will suffer along with the bad people. But God does not tell Habakkuk not to be afraid.

Pray for a calm heart and the ability to deal with fear.

50. HABAKKUK FINDS COMFORT AND STRENGTH

READ: the Book of Habakkuk.

About all that is known of Habakkuk is that he lived when the first Judean captives were carried off to Babylon. The holocaust had begun.

Habakkuk is discouraged and paralyzed by fear. God describes, in the most frightening terms possible, history's first so-called world power. This description could easily apply to any modern power-hungry, land-hungry armed group or nation. Yes, God says, it's true that the Chaldeans' power seems unstoppable and their pride drives them on. Their weapons and idols seem indestructible. But here's the catch. Any group that tyrannizes and oppresses another group will eventually be overthrown by those it oppresses. The Chaldean power will fall through the revolts of the peoples it has conquered.

However, God tells Habakkuk that the Chaldean threat is not irreversible. Habakkuk can do something about it: tell the people of Judah their riotous living, careless morals, and indifference to the rest of the world have moved God to let them be purged by the Chaldeans. Most importantly, there is comfort for those who keep their faith in God.

Then God reminds Habakkuk that He controls everything. This thought astounds, thrills, and comforts Habakkuk. He settles down as he says that no matter what happens, nothing can shake his faith and joy in God's strength.

The Book of Habakkuk tells us in the twentieth century that people in every time have had reasons to be frightened, that through prayer God's people learn to act to correct wrongs, and that they find comfort and strength for hardship through faith in Him.

Thank God for His words to Habakkuk and to us.

51. OBADIAH (1)

. . . and the kingdom shall be the LORD's. Obadiah 21

What's the shortest book of the Old Testament? Obadiah. This book of prophecy has never made memorable reading. So why is it in the Bible?

What did the prophet have to say? And how is his message different from that of the other prophets? Obadiah is something of an individualist. His prophecy is not for the Israelites but for the Edomites, and it is without saving hope for them.

The Edomites, descendants of Jacob's brother Esau, lived in the hilly area southeast of Judah. The jealous rivalry between the two brothers, who had lived more than a thousand years before, continued through their descendants, particularly the Edomites. They'd always harassed the Jews, God's people. When Jerusalem fell to Babylon, the Edomites took advantage, gloating and adding to the Jews' misery.

Edom was a fertile land but had rocky hills, which made good protective fortifications. Alliances with neighboring nations had strengthened the Edomites politically. A major trade route through the country added to their prosperity.

But Obadiah said God would end the Edomites' cruelty to His people, and offense against Him, by causing their destruction. None of their resources would preserve them: not their allies, their rocky fortifications, their prosperity, or their wisdom. Their pride would perish with them.

What is the universal message of Obadiah? The far-reaching effects of prejudice? God's hatred of human pride and cruelty? Proof of God's control of world events? The comfort for God's people in the book's last line?

Pray for God's guidance in your study of the Bible.

52. OBADIAH (2)

READ: the single chapter of Obadiah.

Nothing is known about Obadiah's personal life, only that he wrote after the fall of Jerusalem in 586 B.C. A remarkable thing about Obadiah's prophecy concerning the Edomites is that shortly after he made it, it came true. The trading caravans found other routes, cutting off a source of Edom's wealth. The Assyrians conquered the Edomites and eventually they disappeared. To this day the land is dry and barren. Tourists now visit Petra, its ancient city that has been uncovered by modern archaeologists. Reached through a narrow rocky passage, Petra contains the remains of fabulous buildings carved from the cliffs.

How do I know all this? Not from reading the Book of Obadiah. The Bible is not a complete historical account, nor is it intended to be. But a wealth of historical information is available from other surviving written records and archaeological findings. We can read this information in Bible encyclopedias, concordances, scholarly reports, easy-to-read accounts of Bible lands and cultures, and study guides.

Reading the Bible is difficult, and understanding it sometimes impossible. Outside sources turn the Bible into fascinating reading. More importantly, study aids increase the Bible's meaning and relevance for us.

The basic message of the Bible is clear in selected passages, but most of the Bible becomes clearer with added information. We are fortunate today to have knowledge that enriches our understanding of God through His Word.

Next time you find a part of the Bible you can't comprehend, get a study aid, and enjoy your new discoveries about God.

Praise God for what He teaches us about Himself in His Word.

53. A PRIVATE MATTER

READ: Matthew 6:5–18.

Can anyone force you to pray? Can anything prevent you from praying? Of course not. Why? Because prayer is a private communication between you and God. It cannot be controlled by a third party.

Prayer begins as a need or feeling in your "innermost being," often before you are conscious of it, as a response to something the Holy Spirit plants in you or to something you experience or observe.

When the response becomes a conscious thought, you share it with God and it is a prayer. You tell God what you need. You may praise Him. At the same time God communicates with you. This can happen wherever you are, whatever you're doing.

A prayer is private. It happens because you love God and live close to Him. It's inside your soul. But sometimes the communication with God erupts. You speak out loud, or fall on your knees, or raise your arms, or sing, or cry, or jump and skip. This expression you control, depending on where you are or what you're doing.

Often you need leadership for your prayers. The support of Christians communicating with each other and with God makes a special prayer service.

The motions and words of formal prayer are not the essence of prayer. Someone can force you to go through the formal motion or can prevent it. Do not mistake meaningless formal prayer for inner communication with God.

Rejoice when your prayer communication with God strengthens your bond with Him. Know the joy of praising Him in response to your life's experiences. Your prayer is all yours.

Pray whenever and wherever you have the need.

54. PRAYER CIRCUIT

READ: I Thessalonians 1–2:8.

I once had to complete a large project involving many people. It looked impossible. I became disturbed when I thought of all whom I would disappoint if I failed. But then relatives and friends told me they were praying for me, and knowing they were behind me kept me going until I finished the job.

I was quite young when my father died suddenly. I can't remember the details too well, but I do remember that the power of the prayers of hundreds of people was something our family could feel almost as strongly as we felt our shock and grief.

Now I am writing this book. A friend said she would pray for me. One evening when I felt like giving up I remembered my friend praying for me. It gave me the ambition and the courage to go on. I would not leave her prayer unanswered.

I've been working in a strange town for a couple of weeks. In the small ethnic restaurant where I eat I've become acquainted with the dear foreign-born owner. Business in the new location has been slow, so I've tried to encourage her. This evening as I left, she said, "Thank you for your help. I will pray for you." I decided the Lord really wants me to do this work, because he led me to meet Maria and moved her to pray for me.

I believe prayer is a communal power, something like an electric circuit, coursing through the person praying, God, and the person being prayed for. Prayer is more than one person saying words to God. It includes a response from and responsibility on the part of the person who is the object of the prayer.

Prayer is faith and action by all three parties.

Thank God for people who pray for you.

55. DOES ANYONE CARE?

Cast all your anxieties on him, for he cares about you. I Peter 5:7

Mornings are rough when you wake up dreading the day.

You didn't finish your homework assignment. You'll be teased at your bus stop. You suspect your friends want to dump you. You dread gym class.

Afternoons are rough. Your mom criticizes everything you do. Your brother messes up your room. You're scared of the woman you babysit for, but you need the money.

Evenings are rough. How do you say no to your friends? How do you face that mountain of homework when you want to watch television?

Nights are rough when you can't get to sleep. You regret what you left undone today and dread what you must do tomorrow. The future scares you. You hope that you'll pass, that you'll graduate. You hope there's no war when you're draft age. You hope you'll get a job someday. The world is full of weird things you don't understand.

How can you get relief from these burdens? You pray about them, but nothing changes. Where can you run? Does anyone care?

Deep down you know God cares. He may have already provided help you've overlooked: people close to you. Many people care, and talking to someone who understands eases lots of misery.

Have you tried sharing your feelings with your parents or other family members? You may be surprised to find that they do understand or have the same fears. Do you really have to be afraid of what friends might think if you told them how you feel? They likely have many of the same problems that you do.

Maybe you have to look a bit further—relatives, your pastor, friends at church, a teacher, or a counselor. Someone exists who understands. Someone cares. It's up to you to find the person God has provided for you.

Pray that you will find and have the courage to talk to the person who cares.

56. GO AHEAD, MAKE MISTAKES

READ: I John 1:8–9.

God allows people to make mistakes. Have the courage to learn from yours.

We are puzzled by the Old Testament Israelites who kept repeating the sins for which God chastised them. Why did they do it?

God gave the Israelites the chance to learn from their mistakes. Each tribe and each generation had to find out they depended on God and were important to Him. When they finally refused to see the lessons from their history, God's patience ran out.

In our fear of making mistakes we don't see that mistakes are natural and necessary to living and growing. Schools emphasizing mistakes, parents setting too-high standards for their children, and other people's opinions make people of all ages afraid of making mistakes. Some refuse to take any risks and miss many pleasant and enriching experiences.

Here are some suggestions for handling your mistakes. Be willing to learn from them. Once you make a mistake you seldom make it again. Take it as an opening to finding a better way.

Don't let impatience for an easy way or immediate results keep you from trying something because of the risk of making mistakes. Don't be such a perfectionist that you miss the plain fun of doing things even though you'll make mistakes.

Forgive yourself for your mistakes; they do not make you a worthless person. Put mistakes behind you and move ahead.

Admit mistakes to yourself and to others. Most people don't notice your mistakes as much as you do, and most people are forgiving.

It's the same with God. If we confess our sins He forgives them.

Pray that you will learn from your mistakes.

57. MEMORIAL DAY

READ: Psalm 78:1–7.

Once a year, right before Memorial Day, my mother and I visit my father's grave to place flowers.

Walking through a cemetery makes you think that all that remains of most people is a name on a weathering headstone. Yet everyone was, and remains, more than a name, because everyone has touched someone else. Our present world is the result of what those who lived before us have done. Our bodies and personalities are living inheritances from our ancestors.

The cemetery doesn't seem to me to be the place where my father really is. But when I'm in our high school I'm very much aware of him. He loved that school and devoted much of his energy to it. When he was president of the school board, shortly before he died, the building was dedicated. His work continues to live through that school, and through the children who attend it.

My parents live through me. They passed to me their values, attitudes, knowledge, love, and encouragement. I, in turn, pass them to other children.

The ancient Jews, before the Babylonian exile, did not believe in a life after death. Therefore, they highly valued their children, because they thought that only through their children would they continue to live. The possibility of resurrection was hotly debated during Jesus' day.

To Christians it is unthinkable that there is no life after death. Our salvation through Jesus Christ and hope of resurrection are the foundations of our religion and give meaning to our lives. But we, too, have comfort knowing that our ancestors live through us and that a part of each of us will live through future generations.

Jesus lives. He lives as a name. He lives through us by the knowledge, values, attitudes, and love He passed to us and that we pass to others. Jesus is the resurrected Lord, the living God.

Thank God for the continuity of life through the generations.

58. DAY OF CONTRASTS

READ: I Peter 5:1–5.

This morning I attended a meeting at the university. The committee members were deans, department heads, administrators, and researchers who plan, teach, and help keep the university functioning. All were bright, efficient, confident women with earned doctorates.

I love my new job at the university—learning my way around the campus, using the resources, and, above all, meeting the people, who impress me with their abilities and friendliness. My job stretches my mind and my circle of acquaintances.

The nursing home is near the campus, so this afternoon I went to visit my aunt and deliver her clean clothes. She's a precious little eighty-five-year-old lady, blind, weak, and arthritic. She has no children. She sits in her rocker in a dim corner all day, hardly aware of her surroundings.

She was very confused and distressed today, and her face had a pained expression. Her strange dreams worry her. She'd lost control of her bowels, so the laundry bag was crammed with soiled clothes. When I arrived she'd just had another accident. I talked with her briefly, but she couldn't converse, so I summoned the nurse to change her and quickly drove home to wash her clothes. The chore was not pleasant.

I thought of the day's contrasts: this morning the superior, useful women and this afternoon a humble old lady. It seemed that the Lord was saying, "You may have a nice job with important people who raise your self-esteem, but I have a mess for you to clean up. Your little old aunt is important to Me and I've given her to you to love."

"Okay, Lord," I replied. "You made her to be the way she is, and I'm one of the people You've provided to care for her. Don't let her down."

Pray for the patience you need to love whomever needs your love.

59. THE WAITRESS

READ: Luke 6:20–38.

It was early evening in the elegant restaurant. A quiet ease surrounded the few well-dressed patrons.

Two women were seated at a choice table by the windows. The elderly one was dressed in a dark, heavy, long-sleeved silk dress. She was extremely thin and had an unpleasant rasping voice. Her companion was somewhat younger, too plump for the knit tank top and shorts that revealed a bad sunburn.

The two women were not ill at ease, yet not quite poised. They didn't know what they wanted or how to order. They fussed throughout their meal, the older woman eating very little and the younger one making repeated trips to the salad table. In the subdued restaurant their presence made the other diners uneasy.

The young waitress, besides being genuinely pleasant and patient, made everyone she served feel important. She was particularly friendly to the two unsophisticated ladies.

She asked them about their trip, for they'd come off the highway; she commented sympathetically; she told about herself.

Then something interesting happened. The other patrons began to relax; they stopped resenting the two women, returned to their conversations, and enjoyed their meals.

I was there. My own respect for the women grew.

Perhaps the waitress was well-trained for smart business etiquette. Even so, her respect of lesser persons was a Christian act. She proved that kindness is contagious and a loving manner can transform a whole group of strangers.

Pray for the ability to love everyone.

60. WORK

READ: Ecclesiastes 3:1–15.

Work is on everybody's mind. Unemployment soars, while some jobs go unfilled. Workers worry about being replaced by technology, while employers fret about the inefficiency of their workers. On one hand people measure their worth by the jobs they hold; on the other hand they avoid work. Everyone wants more money. Maybe you're uneasy about your future work.

The Bible honors labor, warns against "slothfulness," and in the Old Testament agricultural setting emphasizes the simple cause and effect of work (Prov. 28:19). The Bible condemns exploitation—forcing someone to work to feed one's own greed (Jer. 22:13–19).

Work was created into the natural order of things, but following God's pronouncement in Genesis 2 people have interpreted work as a hardship, because they have made it self-serving instead of God-serving. Work motivated by greed is always too hard and the rewards never large enough. Many people do not know how to work. They dream of the rewards, but are unable to sustain the minute-by-minute progression of a work day. So they give up.

On the other hand, work has built-in rewards when goals are reached, when jobs are well-done, when work is loving service for others, and when it involves an interesting or pleasant activity.

What can you do about your job future? Practice working. A recently released study shows that the happiest adults were industrious children. Consider work an opportunity to do something worthwhile. The world's work has to be done by someone. Reap the satisfaction of completing your work.

Above all, have service as your goal.

Pray for the motivation to work to serve.

61. BECAUSE GOD SAYS SO

READ: II Timothy 3:14–16.

"Why?" you finally ask your parents in an exasperating argument.

"Because God says so," they answer with disgusting finality. "It's in the Bible."

You're not satisfied, but what can you say to that?

When little kids ask why, they want more information. But you want reason, good sense. Yet when you come up against God's law you have the nagging feeling that reason has hit a stone wall, and you're afraid to question. You give up, but you're unhappy.

But God's laws are not purposeless and unbending. And it's not sacrilegious to question God's rules or try to find sense in them.

God doesn't make laws just to irritate or confine people. His laws have one goal: happiness. God's happiness and ours. He *never* commanded His people to be miserable.

Jesus made the guiding principles—love of God, self, and fellow humans—very clear, and His every word made sense. Paul in his letters expanded Christ's principles into practical terms for the church, and if these statements are read in context they are completely logical.

Some Christians need the security of strict rules and regulations; others find joy in the freedom to try to understand and reason about God's Word. All, however, must be cautious about using selected segments of the Bible to serve only their selfish purposes.

God directs us lovingly, as if to say, "My dear child, this will make you happy, safe, help you to be the loving person you were created to be. Here is how to express your love for Me and make Me happy. I know you couldn't figure it out on your own, so my Word will help you."

Thank God for His laws for our happiness.

62. JOY! NOT GUILTY!

READ: Philippians 4:4–9.

"They" are ruining us. They are trying to convince us it's a horrible world and we are the wretched people whose fault it is. I've had enough! Let's serve notice that we are no longer going to let them pin on us a burden of gloom and guilt.

Who are "they"? In general, negative-minded American adults whose public media and private conversations spout bad news and complaints.

More specifically, "they" are Christians who try loading guilt onto the rest of us.

They make you think you're not a good enough Christian, your faith isn't strong enough, you're not active enough in church. They make you wonder if you're really saved.

They make you think you're bad because you have certain thoughts, or certain tastes in clothing, friends, or entertainment. You never measure up to their standards or expectations. They assume that you have problems you don't have, because they think all teen-agers have them.

They harp so endlessly on society's sins that you feel responsible for them, or guilty because you've not solved them all.

Well, forget them and say good-by to unnecessary gloom and guilt. From now on we're going to be positive and happy, complimentary and encouraging. We will find God's beauty and love around us.

We are on solid ground. God has given us new life in Christ, which means freedom from guilt. That is our joy, the source of our praise, and we would rather praise God than do anything.

Praise God for freedom from guilt and for joy in Christ.